OBSERVATIONS AND SOLUTIONS – THE BARBADOS EXPERIENCE

OBSERVATIONS AND SOLUTIONS – THE BARBADOS EXPERIENCE

Suggestions for Improving Barbados

Trevor Harper

Trevor Harper

Barbados

Observations and Solutions – The Barbados Experience

Suggestions for Improving Barbados

Image on front cover provided by Google earth.

Image on the back cover is a Bearded Fig Tree (*Ficus citrifolia*), the national tree of Barbados.

First Edition

Harper, Trevor
Observations and Solutions – The Barbados Experience

ISBN: 978-1492809302

Printed in the United States of America

To my daughter, Winitry.

CONTENTS

18. Economic crisis could have been avoided

19. In riddance of a pest

20. Crop- Over twice a year

21. Back to the topsy

22. Why an extra finger but not toe?

23. Church, Bible now taking a back seat

24. Barbados the Gem of the Caribbean

25. Which Of Our Famous Landmarks Will Be Next?

26. Let's take the stairs instead

27. Promote more

28. Let's melt their shells

29. The beleaguered boys of today

30. Thou humble Knight

31. Need for parenting classes to stop abuse of children

32. Stuck in the pork line

33. Recession no bother at Christmas

34. Use cameras to catch sugar cane arsonist

Preface

Written by a prolific writer and commentator on social issues affecting Barbados, this book contains intriguing articles with feasible solutions that were published in the local newspapers (Nation and Business Authority) between 2009 and 2013.

The articles are concise and reader friendly, and provide interesting reading with feasible solutions for other countries with societies along a similar developmental path.

1

Democracy or Demockery?

In this Barbadian society - with no offence to anyone - the common man doesn't have a say or input in the decision-making process.

I am mindful of the constituency councils, but top overall decisions that affect our lives and livelihood are made in Parliament and boardrooms without the ideas of the lowest echelons of this society.

Unlike some other societies in the world, where ideas and input are sought and used to make success, it is dismissed here.

God spreads gifts and skills across all echelons. For innovation and rapid improvement to be made in this country, especially in these perilous economic times, we have to be all inclusive.

For even recently in the news, a so- called, self-professed inventor and his worthwhile invention was not recognized and accepted because he did not pass through academia and qualified from there.

Thinking aloud on paper

2

A need to go back to old ways

Owning to the recession, and more so the necessary belt- tightening measures in the recent Budget, Bajans need to go back to the old way of helping each other - by fair exchanges. I believe most would agree.

There was a time when a neighbor reaped or got vegetables, he or she would share them with another neighbor.

If that neighbor had a need for them, conversely, he or she would give in return some vegetables, of which the former was on short supply.

The same would happen with the fruits, protein and carbohydrates.

Motorists would stop and ask of your destination and give you a ride, so long as it was on his or her route. This would also ease the burden of bus fares, in a fair way.

I think the states and the non- government organizations (NGOs) should advocate and encourage this, especially in these austere times. The Government is doing its best and we should as well. Being our brother's keeper is a good start.

3

Stop judging by looks

Looks are still the utmost deciding factor in judgment in Barbados.

Most would remember the case of the unkempt looking prospective customer years ago who went to buy a truck from a company but was ignored because of his looks, but he had the cash.

He went to another dealership and bought it. When the one that turned him down knew of it, the salesman was fired. This perception and attitude still persists today.

How can we improve and get through these perilous economic times with unfair non-developmental exclusions?

We should take a leaf out of the great United States.

4

Don't kick the ladder down behind you

The middle class of a 95 percent (%) black country has emerged in Barbados, where they kick down the ladder of upliftment that has lifted them up.

We still have free and good education, but those who reach a certain high standard of academic qualifications and success exclude others from the decision making and other processes in this country.

Diamonds, gifts and geniuses can be found in any class, academic, race or society. So we should be able to be all-inclusive and not shut others out if you're looking to be innovative, coming together and progressive.

The world is changing in a progressive but also a dangerous way, so we have to find the best ideas and solutions from wherever we can. We need to change our course.

5

COOing all the way to the bank

I saw an article that said that Paradise Beach Ltd (Four Seasons) was looking for a chief operating officer (COO) as opposed to CEO.

A CEO is usually asked to have ten years work experience - five years of which are in management; but the COO request is 15 years' work experience with five years of management.

The position, functions and responsibilities are about the same. But the post name change, as I understand it, means that the person will be ranking in a lot of money.

It also means that he or she will be "COOing" all the way to the bank. It's all in a name.

6

Now is the time to go alone

The recent innuendo by Prime Minister Bruce Golding that Jamaica should establish its own final court of appeal and not accord with the Caribbean Court of Justice (CCJ) further shows the futility of any genuine Caribbean Economy (CSME). Prime Minister Sir Alexander Bustamante, in 1962, started this non- compliance of Jamaica to any unity.

Trinidad and Tobago has done the same thing, starting with the late Dr. Eric Williams (in the Williams-Busamante era), through to Patrick Manning and Kamla Persad- Bissesar wanting to form their own union with some OECS countries, in the face of the CSME, and not wanting to help financially other CSME countries unless there was reciprocation, respectively.

Trinidad won't join the CCJ even though it is headquartered there. And St. Vincent has chided Barbados for priding itself as the best in region - in a negative sense. No regional country seemingly wants to accede to a genuine CSME. So now is the time for each country to go or remain separate and find internal and non- Caribbean initiatives of strengthening the quality of its own people.

7

Remove dangerous trees

In regard to the recent natural downing of a tree at Rockley Beach, Christ Church, it is necessary to remind the relevant authorities that dangerous trees, limbs and branches need to be removed.

An occupied car was destroyed during the incident and could've resulted in very serious injury or even death.

8

Falling down on landmarks

Past and present government administrations have neglected the upkeep of some buildings and trees that are important landmarks in Barbados. Sir Frank Worrell's house, and very recently the tree in the Parliament Yard and another tree at Jubilee Bus Terminal, which were both cut down.

With proper maintenance; watching and treating for wood ants, damage, and so on, these trees could probably still be there, providing shade and adding to the serenity of the area. I wonder which one will be next!

9

Seating and toilets are needed in Baxters Road

While all the improvements made to the traffic light system and food vending facilities in Baxters Roads, the powers that be seem to have forgotten public seating and toilets.

Given the Bajan passiveness and inertia, no one publicly complained. Owing to the dire economic situation, proprietors are reserving their facilities for paying customers only. But there are times when other than a customer might need use of such facilities.

Even tourists have noticed this. Are we going to wait till this is exposed internationally by them? This would be to the detriment of a very important industry.

10

The world - a true global village

We now have the breaking down of trade barriers. Barbados has spread its wings - in terms of tourism, sports , and business and diplomatic, relations - as far as Brazil, East Africa and China. Instant communication, via satellite, Internet, voice, picture, video conferencing, sports and important world events has made the would appear smaller.

But the recent confrontation between Jamaica and the United States - the "Dudus" Coke issue - shows that the US is still getting its way around the world, if Jamaica's prime minister was right when he said that the information the US gave for Coke's extradition request was illegally obtained.

11

Cellphone ban - more loss than gain

With a cellphone, a child can call its parents, the police, and so on, if need be.

He or she doesn't have to look for a pay-phone or ask for a phone call - for that may be too late in the event of a crime on him or her. What if he or she is in a locked room accidentally or purposely or injured, stricken and alone? A cellphone can save a child's life from danger. The mobile provider through its GPS system can track a child's calls and location if need be.

With all these plusses, the mere fact that a child can access or make up pornographic material, to my mind, is not enough to ban cellphones in schools.

In an exam room- yes! But not generally. Porn is easily accessible outside of a cellphone. I say no to banning them in schools.

12

Patriotism also in a name

I think the name Crop Over is outdated and should be changed to Nationfest, Bajanfest or Bajafest.

The Royal Barbados Police Force and the proposed new hospital should be changed to the Barbados Police Force and the name of a great Barbadian doctor, respectively. No offence to the monarchy, but with 43 years of independence, we should show more patriotism in this regard. The radio programme, 'Down to Brass Tacks', should also be renamed 'Up To The People' - though others and I seem to be purposely left out when we called for the last five weeks.

Cou cou and flying fish is not our number one or national dish anymore according to recent newspapers reports. I wonder if it's now the British fish and chips.

13

Dialect does not travel well

Barbadians glorify the negative in theatrical plays, advertisements and so on. It is even done in our use of broken English, like the expression "you is" and so on.

The play 'Bajan Bus Stop', besides the fun, also shows a long wait for the bus. But we don't try to urgently make the necessary positive changes.

"You is" is not Bajan dialect. It's just plain poor English which is sometimes used here and abroad by our educated children, media persons and even our ambassadors. With modern technology, what's on radio, TV, and the Internet goes all over the world, and this kind of exposure is a minus, not a plus for Barbados.

At home "you is" is okay, colloquially, but not in the international media. We need to see and act beyond, for what you practice - "you is" - you'll preach - "you is".

14

Seeing the real problem

We now have reusable bags in supermarkets in Barbados. But the real problem is not the plastic bag itself, but the people; they are the ones who discard them improperly. So you're going to stop selling cars, gasoline and alcohol because of vehicular traffic accident fatalities? They are all people's problems. People need to take control.

15

Toys for Police Force

We now have adult playthings for the Royal Barbados Police Force. The introduction of battery-powered bicycles on the South Coast to help police thwart crime against tourists seems to be providing more fun for the cops than work - for this type of crime is now down.

This is a brilliant introduction by the Prime Minister David Thompson led administration. Because tourism is our number one foreign exchange earner, these battery- powered bikes are a good move, especially in these economically tough times.

I would hasten to add that this is a right path.

16

Ban on kite-flying - an option

Recently, the Barbados Light & Power company Ltd (BL&P) appealed to kite-flyers to desist from flying their kites near power lines. This has been done for years and still continues.

There was also the recent problem of such in Guyana. This also causes power outages - a serious problem for businesses and householders alike. It can even disrupt political and other important meetings.

This practice needs to be stopped, even if it comes down to banning the activity, for there are so many other leisure options available nowadays - unlike when I was growing up - like the internet, the computer, cellphones, video games and so on.

17

Stop negative thinking

Innovation begins with thinking then implementation. But as it relates to the Barbadian experience, we have to erase the impediment in our thinking that products from the United States of America and Europe are best, even when our product is better, agreed to by natives and tourists alike.

Our Banks Beer won an international award many years ago and the Bajan Cherry is best in vitamin C, but a lot of people choose international brands, just because they are from big countries. But be reminded that the very poor and small Haiti was once the Caribbean football champions. The poor and undeveloped beat rich and big USA, Germany and England. Also the West Indies cricket team was once world champions.

We have to remove the negative defeatist thinking that small and poor countries can't achieve and win over big countries, and just do what's needed to be innovative and successful.

18

Economic crisis could have been avoided

The perilous economic situation that the world is experiencing should have never happened. The depression of the late 1920's to 1930's should have been a constant reminder to be more vigilant and to use our more modern financial systems to avert a recurrence of what happened then.

The United States of America with all its money, financial system and brains allowed their commercial banks to be free and careless and to cause this worldwide problem. The US and the world fell asleep on this, resulting on a global financial meltdown. This to me is the ninth wonder of the world.

19

In riddance of a pest

The giant African snail, according to the newspapers late last year, are devouring our food crops at an alarming rate. They were first discovered in 1997 at Brandons, entrance through the seaport, but have now spread to all 11 parishes.

They are negatively impacting on our food import bill which is already high, not to mention the money that is being spent to help eradicate them. Because of the water drought and the dire economic situation, more seriousness and innovation should be applied to this problem. Activate the ministry of innovation in this regard.

20

Crop-Over twice a year

The Crop-Over festival brings in about $80 million a year. So why not have it twice a year?

In these perilous economic times, the big-spending tourists from the north visit mostly in their winter months (tourist season).

So why not have Crop-Over twice - early and later in the year? Maybe we can double up on other festivals as well, making all festivals more attractive.

21

Back to the topsy

In this tough economic time in Barbados, in this water-scare period, we should reintroduce the topsy, so that we wouldn't have to flush thousands of gallons of water every day and night. It would only be for a time

This would not only help the individuals, but the country as a whole, for sometimes in order to go forward, you have to go backwards for a time.

22

Why an extra finger but not toe?

I've noticed that you'll see sometimes a person with an extra little finger but not extra little toes. You'll also see a twin toe but not a twin finger. Why is this so? Maybe medical science can explain this for an inquiring mind.

23

Church, Bible now taking a back seat

With the introduction of Sunday shopping, lots of people who would once before find time to shop outside of Sunday, now use the time that they once took for church to shop. Also, some use time on Sunday for computer and Internet purposes, almost like addicts, paying little or no attention to the church and the Bible.

In this society with declining morals, this absence does not help.

24

Barbados, the Gem of the Caribbean

Barbados has been blessed with the brilliance of world singing sensation Robyn Rihanna Fenty, cricket legend Sir Garfield Sobers, literary great Austin "Tom" Clarke, world draughts champion Ronald "Suki" King, and the world's second oldest living human being James Sisnett.

The country has long been noted as the "Gem of the Caribbean" and righty so. The human rights record is pleasing along with healthcare, but like every country, Barbados has its shortcomings and the negative recessionary interference.

Overall though, all the above-mentioned compel a conclusion that this limestone state of the Bearded Fig Tree, is a bright light in the Caribbean Sea and indeed the world. And fast approaching a world developed small island state (with the various talents abounding) nurtured by successive Governments.

25

Which Of Our Famous Landmarks Will Be Next?

Past and present Government administrations have neglected the upkeep of some building and trees that are important landmarks in Barbados: Sir Frank Worrell's house, and very recently the tree in Parliament Yard and a tree at the Jubilee Bus Terminal, which were both cut down.

With proper maintenance treating against wood-ants, watching for damage and so on, these trees could probably still be there, providing shade and adding to the serenity of the area.

I wonder which one will be next!

26

Let's take the stairs instead

Being mindful of the present Barbadian health situation of having: more than half of our children overweight, an average of three strokes per day, the very high incidence of diabetes and the many amputations relating to it, and the second highest incidence of lupus in the entire world, after Italy, among other serious health challenges, the country should not leave any stone unturned in terms of reversing this health trend.

The elevator should therefore be used only when necessary. It is very well known that exercise is a friend of good health. Conversely, the enemy "continuously eating tasty, but dangerous foods, along with the lack of exercise" - takes one to an early unwelcome grave, leaving spouse, siblings, offspring and friends very aggrieved.

I can see some of our most skillful and innovative citizens passing to the great beyond because of the latter. Putting on my telescopic spectacles, I can further see Barbados' economic growth being stunted by the loss of these very valuable people.

But this does not have to be, for as we all know, appropriate and enough exercise along with proper diet can prevent or drastically reverse the trend.

The county's health authorities and others are doing something: the Browne's Beach exercise and the fun walks and rides. But it's not enough because, on the diet side, proper pork is promoted, encouraged and eaten (pork limes and supermarket advertisements). Macaroni pie and pork dishes have taken over from healthy flying fish and cou cou as our No.1 dish, as recently reported in the newspaper.

It's way past time to stop using the elevator unnecessarily and start promoting a more positive attitude towards changing health habits. Remember, health comes first; any and everything else should be secondary.

27

Promote more

I proudly saw a Barbados Flag at the World Cup. But a flag only showed that a Bajan was there. So were many other countries. Barbados should spend some money advertising our attractions to prospective tourists.

It would cost a pretty dollar, but the gains would outweigh the cost, even if it's only one advertisement.

Likewise, here at home, the World Cup would be a good time for the government to tell and show people how to be innovative in entrepreneurship (there's a ministry of Innovation), as businesses are not hiring.

28

Let's melt their shells

Now that the debate on the giant African snail is raging again, here is my few cents' worth on how to be rid of them.

I would suggest that the authorities develop spray or powder that would dissolve the shells of snails. The snails need them to survive.

I also think it's a good idea for our scientist to find a way to make these giant snails sterile for both male and female lay lots of eggs. The money spent on developing such sterilization would bring much more benefits than that going to all the futile exercises right now.

But are we really serious about getting rid of these ubiquitous giant African snails?

29

The beleaguered boys of today

The debate is still on about co-ed schools. The founding fathers, I think, were wise enough to separate the boys from the girls in education. There were Boys Foundation and Girls Foundation; Harrison College(boys) and Queen's College(girls)

That served us admirably, for boys performed well. But now with co-educational schools the boys are underperforming.

No chauvinism nor disrespect, but girl are definitely a distraction in school. The boys are not going to be thinking mathematics, their minds will be on romantics.

Those who brought co-ed idea to fruition are extremely bright. They are all in a class by themselves.

Maybe they are female chauvinists, for in this co-ed outfit the girls keep outperforming the boys.

30

Thou humble Knight

When most people move from the ordinary to the status of greatness, they become aggrandized and unhumble.

But Barbados' most recent Knight of St Andrew, Sir Branford Taitt, says he is humbled by it, and that he'll remain the same person that he has always been.

He has had a long distinguished career, from Government junior officer, member of the lower and upper house of Assembly, overseas representative, Government minister and cabinet member, through President of the Senate.

Our late great Prime Minister did not reach this rank, and was also humble and down to earth. Maybe we should Knight him as well posthumously. Long live the Knight Sir Branford!

31

Need for parenting classes to stop abuse of children

In the past couple of years I have paid particular attention to child abuse, a crime like adult domestic abuse. Child abuse is not understood by some parents. I've seen it here and abroad as well, where a parent beats a four year old repeatedly for being "hard ears", a Bajan term meaning mischievous, but the child is simply not able to comprehend because of its tender age and immaturity.

Some parents treat children like some teachers do as if they are adults. Some parents even snap at their children and call them "retarded", when the kids are only acting their age. In these cases, the problem lies with the parents; not the child.

I've seen cases where an abused child, even after police Intervention, was still left with the parent. There seems to be no shelter for a child after hours in such cases.

With adult female domestic abuse, the woman is plucked from the circumstance and sheltered; but a child is more vulnerable than an adult.

There's a need for parenting classes as a prerequisite for marriage, foster parenting and the teaching of children.

32

Stuck in the pork line

We are urging our citizens to exercise and exercise more. We also want them to eat healthy.

We have healthy snow-cones (natural juice) and are removing unhealthy snacks from schools. But simultaneously we allowed our number one national dish (flying fish and cou cou), which is healthy, to be supplanted by macaroni pie and pork which are unhealthy.

Barbados has about the world's highest incidence of diabetes and amputations, partly caused by unhealthy eating habits. Oh, what a nagging irony!

33

Recession no bother at Christmas

According to media reports, businesses are seeing Christmas shoppers in the usual numbers or more. Some businesses are even absorbing the Value Added Tax increase.

The $2 and $3 stores have not reduced the Barrels from overseas, even though recession is overseas as well.

Christmas knows no recession, according to the Barbadian experience, and nothing else seems to bother it.

The same goes for the Crop Over festivals. Nothing will stop or prevent a fun time in Bim, not even money... and that's the true Bajan spirit.

No wonder the tourist keep choosing Barbados. We also have the world's No.1 tourist travel information website: Go Barbados.

34

Use cameras to catch sugar cane arsonist

The sugar cane industry is on the wane, with problems from Europe with quotas because of competition from Brazil and Australia. Also through unfavorable rainfall and arson, the yield is lower. So they are planning, and rightly so, to move to a sugar cane industry, which includes the by-products as well.

Sugar was once No.1, now it's tourism. We're protecting this No.1 industry by also using video cameras on the south coast. They are also needed on the west coast. But even though good, they only help catch some criminals after the fact. But we should also use cameras in the cane fields (wide angle cameras that can view over a wide area) to help catch those arsonist as well. This may also deter   them.